Famous Lives

The Story of
SQUANTO
First Friend to the Pilgrims

FAMOUS LIVES
titles in Large-Print Editions:

FAMOUS LIVES

The Story of
SQUANTO
First Friend to the Pilgrims

By Cathy East Dubowski
Illustrated by Steven James Petruccio

Gareth Stevens Publishing
MILWAUKEE

*The author wishes to thank Nanepashemet, Research Associate and Manager
of Native American Interpretation at Plimoth Plantation, for invaluable
suggestions made in reading the manuscript for historical accuracy; and editor
Wendy Wax for her tireless work in seeing the manuscript into print.*

**For a free color catalog describing Gareth Stevens Publishing's list of high-quality books
and multimedia programs, call 1-800-542-2595 (USA) or 1-800-461-9120 (Canada).
Gareth Stevens Publishing's Fax: (414) 225-0377.
See our catalog, too, on the World Wide Web: http://gsinc.com**

Library of Congress Cataloging-in-Publication Data

Dubowski, Cathy East.
　　The story of Squanto: first friend to the pilgrims / by Cathy East Dubowski ;
illustrated by Steven James Petruccio.
　　　　p.　cm. — (Famous lives)
　　Includes index.
　　Summary: Describes how Squanto played an important role in making peace
between his fellow American Indians and the settlers at Plymouth; and the feast
of the First Thanksgiving.
　　ISBN 0-8368-1474-6 (lib. bdg.)
　　1. Squanto—Juvenile literature.　2. Wampanoag Indians—Biography—
Juvenile literature.　3. Pilgrims (New Plymouth Colony)—Juvenile literature.
4. Thanksgiving Day—Juvenile literature.　[1. Squanto.　2. Wampanoag
Indians—Biography.　3. Indians of North America—Massachusetts—Biography.
4. Pilgrims (New Plymouth Colony).　5. Thanksgiving Day.]　I. Petruccio, Steven,
ill.　II. Title.　III. Series: Famous lives (Milwaukee, Wis.).
E99.W2S624　1997
974.4'82004973'0092—dc20
[B]　　　　　　　　　　　　　　　　　　　　　96-30712

This edition first published in 1997 by
Gareth Stevens Publishing
1555 North RiverCenter Drive, Suite 201
Milwaukee, Wisconsin 53212 USA

Original © 1990 by Parachute Press, Inc., as a Yearling Biography. Illustrations © 1990 by
Steven James Petruccio. Published by arrangement with Bantam Doubleday Dell Books
for Young Readers, a division of Bantam Doubleday Dell Publishing Group, Inc.
Additional end matter © 1997 by Gareth Stevens, Inc.

1 2 3 4 5 6 7 8 9 01 00 99 98 97

Contents

A Note to the Reader

Most of what we know about Squanto we learned from the English explorers and colonists who knew him. These people wrote only of how Squanto affected their lives and little of his life away from them. The Indians did not have a written language, so there are no written Indian records of Squanto's birth or life or thoughts. There is a lot about him that we will never know for certain. We can only guess.

In addition, stories about the Pilgrims have been told over and over. We have heard them for so long that they seem almost like fairy tales. Sometimes stories were exaggerated, and sometimes facts were changed. In the stories of Thanksgiving, Squanto is a hero. He helped the Pilgrims plant corn so they would not starve. He helped make peace between the Pilgrims and the Indians.

But Squanto was more than a hero in a holiday legend. He was a real person. Some things we know for sure about him. Other things may or may not be true.

What *do* we know for sure about Squanto? We believe he was born sometime in the late 1500s, although the exact year is not certain. A lot has been learned about what life was like then for Indians who lived in southern New England, where Squanto was from. We know that he spent several years in England. And much has been written about the time he spent with the Pilgrims.

We also know that his name was really Tisquantum (tih-SKWAN-tum).

European explorers were not used to the languages of the Native American peoples. Sometimes they were not sure how to write down Indian words using English letters. Different people often wrote down the same names or words in different ways. Sometimes the writers were careless, and the words they wrote down did not sound at all like the Indian words.

William Bradford, Plymouth Plantation's second

governor, wrote a book called *History of Plymouth Plantation*. He heard the name *Tisquantum* and wrote it down as *Squanto*. Since much of what we know about Tisquantum comes from this book, we have come to know this man by the Pilgrims' name for him: Squanto.

We may not be able to fill in every detail of Squanto's life. But we do know enough about him to tell the story of the very important role he played in the history of America.

A Boy Named Tisquantum

Late one night about four hundred years ago a young Indian boy lay awake on his low wooden bed covered with furs. The night was cold, but he was warm by the fire that glowed in the center of his wetu (WEE-too). Wetu is an Indian word for a dome-shaped building that was covered with mats made of straw, reeds, or bark. The wetu was the Indian boy's home. All around him he heard the low, soothing voices of his people. They were singing themselves to sleep.

But on this night the boy was not sleepy. Wide awake, he watched smoke from the fire rise through the opening at the top of the wetu, and caught a glimpse of stars shining brightly in the clear, cold sky.

The boy's name was Tisquantum, and he belonged to the Wampanoag (WOM-puh-NO-ug) tribe. Wampanoag is an Indian word that means "eastern people." The Wampanoag lived in many villages throughout what would one day be southeastern Massachusetts and eastern Rhode Island. Tisquantum lived in a coastal village called Patuxet (Pa-TUCK-set), near Cape Cod Bay. The people in each village were known by the name of their village. So Tisquantum and the 2,000 other Indians who lived there were called the Patuxet.

The Patuxet lived from nature. They fished and hunted and farmed, making the most of the natural resources of each season. They had a central village that was their main home. But sometimes the Patuxet would leave the village to live in nearby areas where food was the most plentiful.

In the spring, herring swam upstream to lay their eggs. Wild birds that had flown south for the winter began to return to the area around Cape Cod. Every year at this time, Tisquantum and the other Patuxet moved to the rivers to fish and hunt and give thanks that nature had provided so much food.

When the days grew warmer, it was time to plant. Then the Patuxet families moved into summer we-tus near the fields. The women planted Indian corn, beans, pumpkin, and squash. They also gathered skunk cabbage and blackberries that grew wild in the woods. The men hunted bears, deer, beavers, and wild turkey. Sometimes the children played and sometimes they helped the women in the fields. The men and boys played games that were much like soccer. The men also loved to gamble for blankets or furs with dice made out of bone.

The Patuxet harvested much more food than they could eat. Much of what they grew or gathered was dried. Drying food was a way to keep it good for many months. That way the Patuxet could store it for the winter, when it would be too cold for fresh crops.

At summer's end, the women harvested the fields. They dried the corn that would feed their families throughout the winter. Then they stored the corn in deep holes lined with mats made of rushes.

After the harvest, the Patuxet moved back to the central village. The nights grew cold. Birds flew south for the winter. Fresh game was harder to find. It was time for the long hunt.

During the long hunt the men traveled far from the village to hunt deer. For days they lived in bark-covered hunting wetus. The older sons went to learn to hunt. The wives and older daughters of the tribe went, too. They cooked for the men. When the hunters killed a deer, the women dried the meat and scraped the hides. If the hunt was good, there was lots of meat. And there were many skins to make into clothes and blankets.

Every year of his life Tisquantum had watched the hunting party leave without him. Since Tisquantum was still a boy, he had not yet gone with the men on their long hunting trips. Every year he had stayed in the village with the children and the elders.

It was not *all* bad to stay behind. The white-haired elders of the village taught Tisquantum and the other Patuxet boys how to make tools. Young girls were taught how to weave grass mats. Gathered around the fires at night, they amused the children with stories. Over and over again, they repeated the legends and traditions of the Wampanoag people until the children knew them by heart.

The Wampanoag had no written language, no books to read. But the elders were like living books.

By telling stories of their past, and of nature, the elders taught the children important lessons. And one day, the Patuxet children would tell *their* children the same stories. This was how they learned, instead of going to school.

How Tisquantum laughed at the tale of why the cricket is black! He listened in awe as he heard the story of how the first man and woman were made from a tree.

The elders were wise and patient teachers. In return for their help, Tisquantum and the other children looked after the elders with great love and respect when they were too old to care for themselves.

Tisquantum learned many important lessons in the village. But there would come a day when he would join the men on the long hunt. One day soon he would have the chance to prove what a fine hunter he had become. Like the other boys in the village, he had learned to hunt as soon as he could hold a bow and arrow. He also knew how to use spears and traps to catch fish.

Just as important, he had learned to walk silently through the forest. He had studied the ways of the animals so he could catch them more easily. The elders had taught Tisquantum to respect all living

creatures. They had taught him to apologize to an animal after taking its life. When he hunted, it was always to feed his people—never just for sport.

How proud his family was of him when he brought squirrels and rabbits for the family's cook pot! Their praise filled Tisquantum with happiness.

When he misbehaved, Tisquantum was not spanked. Instead he had to bear the stern displeasure or disappointment in his parents' eyes. To a Wampanoag child, knowing that he had let his parents down was far worse than a beating.

All the boys in Tisquantum's village were raised to be strong and tough. They were taught to face pain and hardship bravely, without crying or grumbling. They learned to control their feelings and discipline themselves. These things were a sign of strength. The Wampanoag believed that boys had to be strong before they could become men. Each boy must accomplish some "notable act"—such as tracking and killing a deer—to pass into manhood.

The training of some boys was even harder than this. This was because these boys were chosen to be pnieses (puh-NEES-es). A pniese held an honored place in the village because he had the power to call on a spirit power called Hobbamock (HOB-uh-mok). The Indians believed this god held great power. A pniese had the special job of appealing to Hobbamock to protect his people—or to send trouble to their enemies! Even the village's chief, or sachem (SAY-chem) treated a pniese as special. Only a few boys were chosen for such a great honor.

Tisquantum was eager for the day when he would face the test of manhood. He wanted to prove his courage to all the village and show that he had become strong in mind and body.

He never imagined he would not live his whole life among the Patuxet. For generations life in his village had been the same. But now things were changing.

Tisquantum and his family had heard stories from tribes who lived to the north. Strange men with white skin had crossed the ocean in huge ships! They came from faraway places with names that meant nothing to the Indians—names like England and France.

At first the white men came to fish or trade for furs. Some came to hunt for gold and other treasures. Tisquantum did not know that as he grew older, more and more white men would come. In a few years they would start to bring their wives and children, too. They would seek to make new homes for themselves on the rich land where only Indians had lived before.

One day Tisquantum himself would sail across the great waters in one of the white men's big ships! English families would make their home on the very land he now slept upon! They would write about Tisquantum in their books. Long after he was dead, more people than Tisquantum had ever dreamed of would know about him and his life. But as Tisquantum the boy lay in his warm, snug wetu, he could not foresee any of this. For now, as the singing voices of his people faded into the night, Tisquantum dreamed only of the hunt.

Kidnapped!

Many years later, on a fine day in late summer, Tisquantum was walking along the sparkling waters of the bay not far from his home. He had grown into a fine strong man and had taken his place among the men of the tribe.

Suddenly Tisquantum froze in his tracks. He was surrounded by white men.

As a boy Tisquantum had heard many stories of these foreigners. He may have seen a Frenchman named Samuel de Champlain when he and his crew explored and mapped the bay nearly ten years before. Only recently an Englishman named John Smith had visited these shores and traded with some of his people. Now Tisquantum was surrounded by white strangers. But the tall, strong Indian showed no fear.

How strange they looked! The weather was hot. Tisquantum wore only a loincloth about his waist and leather moccasins on his feet. But these men covered their bodies from head to toe with many layers of clothing. Even their faces were covered with hair! At their sides gleamed fine knives—each as long as a man's leg. The knives the Patuxet used were not half so large.

Tisquantum listened as the men spoke to him. He could not understand their excited, mysterious words, but they wore smiles of friendship. Other white men had come to trade with the Patuxet— perhaps these men also wanted to trade.

The men waved their arms about and pointed to the bay. When Tisquantum looked, he saw a big, fine ship floating on the blue water. What a dazzling sight! The boats of Tisquantum's people were small dugout canoes made from a single tree. They were sleek and could slip silently along the woodland streams and rivers. But this boat was huge. It was made of dozens of trees. Just think of how many people it could carry!

The leader of the white men was Captain Thomas Hunt. Captain Hunt and his men had come to the New World with Captain John Smith, who was exploring the New England coast from Maine to Cape Cod. When Captain Smith returned to England, Captain Hunt was supposed to finish up fishing the rich waters of the New World and take his catch to Málaga, Spain. But he was a greedy man. He had other ideas.

Captain Hunt and his men lured Tisquantum onto their ship. Once there, Hunt and his men lost their friendly smiles. They grabbed Squanto and locked him up with chains. Then they threw him down into the hold of the ship. He was a prisoner! Nineteen other Patuxet were captured this way, too.

Tisquantum lay in the dark hold of the ship with no way of knowing what was to become of him. He talked with the other Indians. All were stunned by what the English had done. Why were they in chains? What did Captain Hunt plan to do with them? Imagine how terrifying it was! But these were brave Indian men, and they did not show their fear—not even when the ship began to move!

The ship rocked and dipped as it sailed through the waters. Soon it stopped again. Tisquantum and the others waited and waited. At last the door to the hold opened, and light spilled into the gloomy pit.

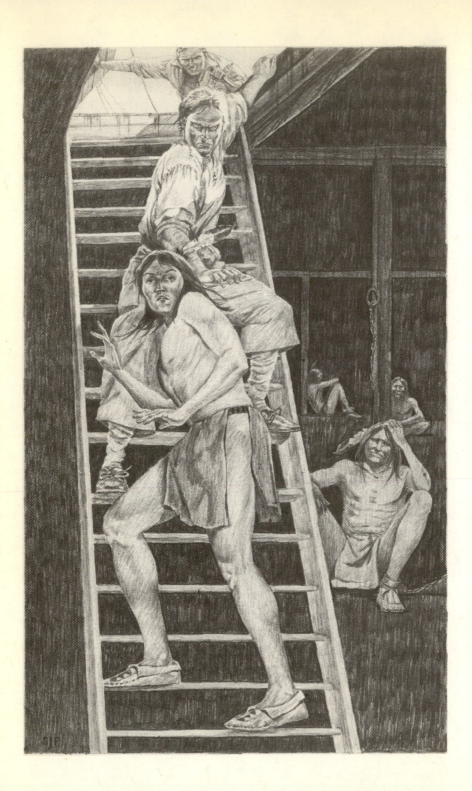

Seven more Indians were thrust below. Then the door slammed shut and it was pitch dark once more.

Tisquantum spoke with the new captives. They, too, were Wampanoag Indians, from the village of Nauset (NAH-set). They did not know any more than Tisquantum of what the English were going to do with them.

Above them, the voices of sailors calling to one another rang out. Soon the Indians felt the rocking of the ship as it began to move again. The ship picked up speed, plunging through the waves.

Captain Hunt's ship was heading out to sea!

They sailed for days, for weeks. Captain Hunt was taking Tisquantum and the other Indians farther away from their villages than any of them had ever been. He was taking them all the way across the Atlantic Ocean to Europe!

Many Indians had been taken to Europe before. Explorers took them there to show off what the New World was like. These explorers would sometimes rent a stage and set up an Indian show. Someone would stand outside and shout, "Come see the savages from the New World!" People would pay money to come and stare at the Indians.

The explorers hoped Indian shows would make people interested in learning more about the New World. They used the Indians to raise money to help pay for their trips to explore and trade there.

Most explorers also tried to show their captured Indians how wonderful the English ways were. They wanted the Indians who returned to the New World to tell their people how good and friendly the English were. That way, the Indians would want to keep trading with the English.

But there were many English people who thought that taking Indians against their will was a bad idea. They thought it would make the Indians hate the English. That would mean it would become even harder for the English to explore and trade.

At last Captain Hunt's ship reached land. Tisquantum had spent many long weeks in the ship's dark hold. He and the other Indians had hardly ever been allowed up on deck for fresh air. They were not used to sunlight anymore. Now the bright warm sun hurt their eyes as they stepped out on deck and looked around.

The land where Captain Hunt had brought them was hot and sunny. Tisquantum could not understand the words of the people as he was taken into the streets. Even worse, he and the others were still in chains.

Never before had any of them seen buildings of brick and stone—with rooms on top of each other! There were so many of them, and they were built so close together. The streets were filled with people coming and going. Tisquantum had never heard church bells before. But here, bells rang out into the air all the time. He marveled at the strong shining animals he saw people riding—he had never seen horses before!

What would happen to them in this strange place?

Captain Hunt had brought Tisquantum and the others to Málaga, Spain. He was going to sell his fish catch here. But Hunt had plans for his Indian captives, too.

He was going to sell them as slaves!

A Slave and a Servant

One by one the Indians were put up for sale. Each proud brave had to stand before a crowd and let people look him over as if he were an animal! Many of the people had never seen Indians before. They touched and poked at them to see what their hair felt like or what their clothes were made of.

There were no laws to stop Captain Hunt from selling his prisoners for whatever price he could get. And people were eager to buy slaves from the New World. Several Indians were sold right away.

Suddenly the noisy mob fell silent. All eyes turned from the Indians to the edge of the crowd. Several men in long brown robes had appeared.

These men were Catholic monks. The Catholics had been very powerful in Spain for a long time. Many people were afraid of them. The crowd parted to let the monks pass. Some people bowed to show their respect.

The monks were angry that Captain Hunt was selling the Indians. They believed it was wrong. They ordered the captain to stop.

With gentle smiles the monks led the unsold Indians away to be instructed in the Christian religion. They had been rescued!

Was Tisquantum rescued? Or had he already been sold as a slave? It's a mystery—no one knows for sure. What we do know is that at last he made his way to England on a ship. Perhaps he was sold to the ship's master. In this way he may have been passed from hand to hand many times.

Somehow, at last, he came to live with a man named John Slany in the great English city of London.

Slany was a wealthy man who worked for the Newfoundland Company, a company that traded and explored in the New World. Tisquantum may well have worked as Slany's servant to earn his keep.

Everywhere Tisquantum went people crowded around him. Most English people had heard tales of the wild "savages" who lived across the ocean. But many had never seen an Indian in real life.

Everything was new and different to Tisquantum at first. English beds were soft and high off the ground. They were nothing like the low, wooden beds he had slept on in Patuxet. Tisquantum now wore English clothes—shirts, pants, coats, hats, and even stockings. They were more confining than the deerskin clothes he was used to. And they covered him from head to toe—even in summer! By now, Tisquantum knew a little English. But in London, he saw many things for which he did not even have a name in his own language.

Every day there were new things to see. There were English clocks and new English foods to try. And there were books and paintings and ships from around the world.

Slowly Tisquantum learned the English words for all these things. He would point to the food on his plate and someone would say "bread." Squanto would repeat the new word. He would say it again and again until he knew it by heart. Word by word, he learned the Englishmen's language. He also learned their manners. Their way of doing business. Their way of thinking.

The people around him talked often of politics

and religion. It was a troubled time in England. Many of the people were poor. Others were unhappy because they did not have the freedom to worship in their own way.

In England only one religion was allowed. This was the Church of England, and it was headed by King James I. Not everyone agreed with the Church of England, but to go against the church was to go against the king or queen. It was treason! Anyone who followed another religion could be punished by their neighbors or by the king's soldiers.

One group of people who dared to worship a different way were called Puritans. Some Puritans were known as Separatists, because they had separated completely from the Church of England. They did not believe the king should rule the church. They did not believe in fancy church buildings or showy worship services. They wanted to create a simpler church that was based only on what the Bible told them to do.

The Separatists had heard the tales of the New World. Maybe they could follow their own religion there. This gave the Separatists hope. They began to make plans to go to the New World.

*　　*　　*

Tisquantum, too, would leave England before long. In 1618, John Slany sent him to Newfoundland. Newfoundland is an island off the Atlantic coast of what is now Quebec Province, Canada. Slany's Newfoundland Company did a lot of trading there, and he thought Tisquantum could help. Tisquantum had learned to understand and speak English. He could work as a translator, helping the Englishmen and the Indians to understand each other.

In Newfoundland, Tisquantum met a man named Captain Thomas Dermer. Captain Dermer worked for Sir Ferdinando Gorges, an English explorer. Dermer was enchanted by Tisquantum's stories of Patuxet. It sounded like such a wonderful place that he decided to see it for himself.

Captain Dermer wanted to travel south to Tisquantum's native land with Tisquantum as his guide. So he took Tisquantum back to England to meet Gorges and ask for permission to make the trip.

Gorges wanted to colonize New England. How useful it would be to have a Native who could speak English so well. Tisquantum seemed to understand the English people, too. Gorges knew that greedy explorers such as Captain Hunt had made many

Indians distrust the English. Some Indians had been taken as slaves. Others had been killed. To be successful in the New World, the English had to win back the trust of the Indians. Maybe Tisquantum could help.

Here was Tisquantum's chance to return to his people. He agreed to go with Captain Dermer, and plans for the trip were made. A crew was hired. Food and other supplies were bought and packed into the ship.

Finally, in March of 1619, Tisquantum stood on the deck of another huge English ship. Captain Dermer shouted out orders to prepare the ship to sail. The crew whistled and sang as they unfurled the sails and pulled the anchor from the water. At last the ship sailed out across the waves.

After nearly four years away from Patuxet, Tisquantum was going home!

After several weeks, Captain Dermer's ship reached New England, along the coast of what one day would be Maine.

Tisquantum did well as Captain Dermer's guide. He spoke to the Indians and gave them the captain's words of peace. Both the Indians and Captain Dermer had to trust Tisquantum to translate their messages correctly. It took great skill to think in both languages at the same time—and to make sure one side did not accidentally offend the other. Tisquantum was proud to do such important work.

The exploring party traveled farther south, closer and closer to Patuxet. At last their travels brought them to Cape Cod Bay. Tisquantum recognized the place at once. Even though it had been four long years since he had walked the beaches that ran along the bay, or followed the well-worn trails through woods, Tisquantum had never forgotten his people.

How he longed to see his home once more. But as Tisquantum neared his old village of Patuxet, he sensed that something was wrong. He saw no sign of hunters in the woods. No children ran along the paths to greet him. The trails were choked with weeds, as if no one had used them in a long time. He did not smell the smoky campfire his people always kept burning.

A chill ran through Tisquantum's heart. As far north as Maine, he and Dermer had heard of a great sickness—a plague—which had killed many Native people in many villages throughout New England. Had the plague come to his village?

Tisquantum ran to the clearing in the woods

where the main village had been. After so many years in England he still knew the way with his eyes closed. But as he looked around, he could not believe what he saw.

His people were all gone!

Alone

Tisquantum looked around, stunned. The wetus had all been deserted and fallen into decay. No one had lived in the village for some time. The nearby fields had not been planted. Tisquantum searched through the woods for clues where the Patuxet might be.

He found nothing.

What had happened to his people? What had happened to his family?

The explorers decided to travel farther inland. Perhaps, among the people of other Wampanoag villages, they could find someone who knew what had happened to the Patuxet.

They found answers in a village called Namasket

(Nuh-MAS-kit), a full day's journey inland. From there Dermer sent a messenger to a village called Pokanoket (puh-KON-uh-ket), another day's journey to the west.

Soon two Indian kings with fifty armed men came to confer with him. These "kings" were probably Massasoit (Mass-uh-SO-it) and his brother Quadequina (KWAH-duh-KWEE-nuh). Massasoit was the powerful chief—or sachem—of Pokanoket and held great influence over other Wampanoag communities.

From Massasoit and Quadequina, Tisquantum heard the story of what had happened to his people.

Two winters before, the great plague had reached the village of Patuxet. Almost everyone had died. Those who did not die had left the village. They carried the sickness to the other Wampanoag villages. Many of the Pokanoket had died, too. Once the Wampanoag had been a strong people of more than 20,000. As many as half had died in the plague.

Such plagues had not happened in New England before. European explorers brought many new diseases to the New World—diseases such as smallpox, chicken pox, and measles. The Indians had never been exposed to these diseases. Since they did not know how to fight or cure them, many people died.

The Wampanoag had suffered greatly because of the plague. Now, they were so few that their enemies held greater power over them. Most feared were the Narragansett (NAR-uh-GAN-set) Indians, who lived to the west. Why had their gods allowed them to become so weak in the face of their enemies? Many must have wondered.

Tisquantum continued with Dermer's expedition. But when Dermer decided to go to Virginia, Tisquantum stayed behind on the coast of Maine, near the Saco River. Perhaps he hoped to find survivors of the plague that had struck his people.

Without Tisquantum, Captain Dermer's travels had nothing but trouble. Many Indians had learned to distrust European explorers. They had seen too many of their people hurt or captured. Once, some Englishmen had even lured Indians onto a ship and shot them for no reason. Such actions made these Indians hate white men. They greeted whites as enemies, not as friends.

Captain Dermer was captured several times by Indians after Tisquantum left him. Each time he managed to escape. In the summer of 1620, he returned to New England and once again talked Tisquantum into serving as his guide as he continued his exploration southward. Another Indian, named Samoset, may also have come along.

Later that summer Captain Dermer was taken prisoner once again. This time he was captured by the people of Pokanoket and Namasket, the people he had met with peacefully the summer before, when they told Tisquantum of the plague that had killed his people. Only when Tisquantum spoke on the Englishman's behalf did the Indians set him free.

Together Tisquantum and Dermer traveled to Martha's Vineyard, an island to the south of Cape Cod Bay. But on Martha's Vineyard, they met another Indian who saw Dermer as a threat.

The Indian's name was Epenow (EE-pen-now). Epenow had once been captured by an English explorer named Nicholas Hobson and taken to Sir Ferdinando Gorges. He had escaped from explorer Edward Harlow in 1614, the same year Tisquantum was kidnapped and taken to England. Now Epenow hated all white men. He believed that they were evil and would destroy the Indians. And he feared that they would capture him again.

Dermer had actually met Epenow once before

and had had no trouble. But this time Epenow and his men attacked Captain Dermer's party. Many of Dermer's men were killed. The captain himself was wounded, but managed to escape to Virginia, where he later died of his wounds.

Tisquantum and Samoset were captured by Epenow. Even though Tisquantum was an Indian, Epenow did not trust him because he was helping Captain Dermer. Epenow made Tisquantum and Samoset his prisoners and took them to Pokanoket. There, Epenow turned them over to the Pokanoket chief, Massasoit. Once again, Tisquantum was being held captive—this time by Indians!

As a boy, Tisquantum had learned to bear hardship without emotion. As a man he had endured kidnapping and had lived in strange lands. He had learned to make the best of his situation.

Now he hoped to make things better for himself by becoming valuable to Massasoit. He knew the chief was worried because his tribe was weaker than their enemy, the Narragansett. Tisquantum told Massasoit he knew of a way to make the Pokanoket strong again.

Tisquantum sat with Massasoit before the fires at night. He charmed the chief with stories of all he had seen in Europe. There were many, many English people, he said, and many English soldiers. The English people had great knowledge and power. Massasoit should make friends with them. With such powerful friends, said Tisquantum, Massasoit's enemies would have to bow down before him.

Tisquantum told the chief that he could be of special help in befriending the English. Tisquantum knew the English ways and language. No Indian would be better able to talk with them than he was.

Massasoit listened to his prisoner and agreed. Tisquantum could indeed help his tribe to become strong again.

A few months later Tisquantum would have a chance to prove his worth.

It was November of 1620. The harvest was in. The days grew short, and the nights grew cold. Soon the snows would come. The men in the village began to talk of the long hunt.

Suddenly exciting news spread among the Pokanoket people. An English ship had laid anchor at Cape Cod. Only this time the ship did not bring men to fish or trade for furs. This ship brought women and children.

Tisquantum listened to the news of the ship's arrival with great interest. This was the chance he was waiting for. Soon he would visit these English. Then he would amaze Massasoit and the Pokanoket people with his great skill in dealing with the white men.

Tisquantum would have to be patient, however, because the Pokanoket decided not to greet the newcomers right away. To make friends with the English was a very serious step. The Indians would find out what the English were up to before they made their move. For now, they would watch and wait.

Saints and Strangers

In November of 1620, a big ship called the *Mayflower* landed at Cape Cod, on the coast of New England. The people on board the *Mayflower* had come to make a new home for themselves in the New World. They hoped to have more freedom and opportunity here than they had had in England.

For years they had planned their journey. They had dreamed of the land where all their hopes for a better future lay. They had collected everything they would need to start their new home: food and clothing, gunpowder, and tools. Every corner of their ship was stuffed with these things. There would be no stores in the New World, no town to welcome them. There would be no homes ready to live in, or fields already harvested. They would have to do everything themselves. And ships bringing supplies would be rare.

In all, there were fifty men, twenty women, and thirty-two children. They had left Plymouth, England, in September. For sixty days they had been at sea, and the trip was long and hard. The *Mayflower* had come through many storms. There had been no heat and little to eat but cheese and dried fish and a kind of bread called hardtack. There was little privacy and little to do to fill the long hours of each day.

But there had been joy on the ship, too. A baby boy had been born while the *Mayflower* was at sea. He was named Oceanus, because he'd been born on the ocean.

Now these men and women and children looked upon the New World for the first time. It seemed stark and wild. Had they made the right choice in coming here?

These were the people who became known as the Pilgrims. But they did not call themselves that. In fact, two different groups came over on the *Mayflower*. One group called themselves Saints. They were Puritan Separatists, and they were in charge of the journey. They had braved the risky voyage so they could make their own rules and worship God in their own way.

The Saints called all the others who had made the trip Strangers. Some of the Strangers had come to the New World to make their fortunes. Others were hired hands or servants.

The Saints and the Strangers had not always gotten along on the voyage. Now that they had arrived in New England, the arguments grew even worse. The leaders of the small group knew that they needed to work together if they were to survive in this wild place. Fighting among themselves could destroy them.

In order to keep the peace, the Saints sat down and wrote up an agreement. In it, they promised to make and follow fair laws. They also chose a governor, a Saint named John Carver. This agreement was known as the Mayflower Compact, and it was the first written law in America. All the adult male Saints and Strangers signed it.

The next thing the Saints and Strangers had to do was to find a place where they could build their new home. For now they continued to live onboard the *Mayflower*. Each day a few men went out in a small open boat called a shallop to hunt for a good

spot. They were led by a Stranger, a soldier named Captain Miles Standish. He was short and had bright red hair. And he grew red in the face when he was angry—which was often!

Captain Standish and his men feared being attacked by Indians. Sometimes they felt as if someone were watching them, but when they looked into the thick trees they saw no one. Once they glimpsed six Indians with a dog far down the beach. But when the colonists walked toward them, the Indians disappeared into the woods.

Days passed and still the Pilgrims did not find a good, safe place to settle. But they did make some useful discoveries. During one of their trips Captain Standish and his men found strange mounds of earth. They dug them up and discovered they were graves.

Farther on they dug up another mound and found two woven baskets each filled with three or four bushels of colorful Indian corn. They also found a huge black kettle that must have come from Europe.

What luck! They could plant the corn as seed in the spring. Several men formed a circle to stand guard while two or three men dug up the basket of corn. If they ever met the owners, they said, they would surely pay them for it. Before leaving, they named the place Cornhill.

On another trip they found two empty wetus filled with earthen pots, baskets, several deer heads, and dried fish. The men took some of the best things with them. Perhaps later they could return with some beads and leave them in the houses as payment and a sign of peace.

The search for a home continued, hampered by cold, rainy weather. The rest of the Pilgrims spent most of the time onboard. Imagine how hard it must have been to wait and wait, now that they had reached land. One day a restless young boy named Francis Billington got into trouble playing with a fowling gun in his father's cabin. A spark from the gun ignited a barrel of gunpowder and nearly set the ship on fire!

One dark evening, around midnight, the scouting party awoke to the sound of horrible cries in the night! "To arms! To arms!" the man on guard shouted. The men grabbed their muskets and fired several times into the dark night sky. The noise stopped. The men decided the cries must have been made by wolves.

But early the next morning, as the men prepared

their breakfast, they heard the same terrifying cries. One of their men came running from the woods. "They are men! Indians! Indians!" he cried. Soon the air was filled with flying arrows.

The men scrambled for their muskets. Soon after they began firing the Indians disappeared into the woods. The Pilgrims thanked God that none of them had been wounded. They gathered up some of the arrows to send to England. They called it their "first encounter," and the place became known as "First Encounter Beach."

Finally, on December 26, the Pilgrims found what one of them called "a most hopeful place," named Plymouth on the maps made by the explorer Captain John Smith. There was already a nice clearing sheltered by woods. The soil was rich, and the water sparkling clean. The woods were filled with herbs and nuts and berries they could eat. It seemed to be the perfect spot!

There was something strange about the place, however. It looked as though people had once lived there. Near the clearing, the Pilgrims found what seemed to be fields. But they were deserted and overgrown. If anyone *had* lived there, the Pilgrims decided, they had been gone for a long time. It would be all right to build their homes here. They would call their settlement Plymouth Plantation. Little did the Pilgrims know that their new home was exactly where Tisquantum's boyhood village of Patuxet had been.

By now the cold, wintry weather had really set in. Many of the Pilgrims were getting sick. It was more important than ever to build shelter. Some of the men went ashore each day to chop down trees to use in building houses. Others gathered reeds to make thatch for the roofs.

Slowly the Pilgrims made progress. First they built a large Common House. Those who worked ashore lived there while they began building the individual houses.

It was actually a rather mild winter by New England standards, with very little snow. But the cold rainy weather made it difficult to work. Sometimes the weather was so bad the Pilgrims couldn't work for several days at a time. There was very little food. Nearly everyone fell sick.

In December, six of the Pilgrims died. As the winter wore on, sometimes two or three people died in a single day. Many mornings only a handful of the settlers were well enough to get out of bed.

These few had to fetch all the wood and keep all the fires going. They had to cook and clean, and nurse the sick.

By March, nearly fifty people had died. That was half of the colony. Only four of the grown women survived. Many children were left orphans. Surprisingly, only three of the children died—all boys. The parents, especially the brave mothers, must have gone without food so their children would live.

This was not the life the Pilgrims had planned for their children in the New World. They had known that the first years would be hard ones. But the reality of the difficult challenge dampened their dreams. They did not want to give up and go home. But even if they did, there was no way the *Mayflower* could make the dangerous ocean voyage in winter. All they could do was hope and pray that God would help some of them live until spring.

The Pilgrims had other worries, too. Now they knew for sure that the woods were filled with Indians. Sometimes at night they saw the distant smoke of Indian campfires. Once in a while they saw Indians in the distance. Through that bleak winter the Pilgrims waited for the cover of darkness to bury their dead. They did not want the Indians to know how small and weak their group was becoming.

The Pilgrims did not know what the Indians were thinking or planning. But they knew that the Indians were watching. And this scared them.

"Welcome, English!"

All that winter the people of Pokanoket were indeed watching the English. They were waiting for the right time to show themselves to these white settlers. They knew things were not going well, and that the English were weak. This meant that the chief of the Pokanoket tribe, Massasoit, would have the upper hand when he finally met them.

In March of 1621, Massasoit decided it was time to move. The Pokanoket would befriend the English and win them as allies.

The first step was to send someone to greet the English, someone who knew their language. Both Tisquantum and the Indian who had come from

Maine named Samoset could speak English. Both had spent time with English-speaking people. But Tisquantum could speak the language much better than Samoset. He had lived in England while Samoset had not. Tisquantum was the most valuable messenger.

Chief Massasoit did not want to send his best translator, however. He could not be sure of what the English would do. They might capture or kill an Indian who went to their settlement. Massasoit did not want to risk losing Tisquantum, so he sent Samoset to the English first.

On Friday, March 16, 1621, many of the Pilgrims were still sick. No one was on guard watching for danger. What a shock it was to them when Samoset boldly walked into the middle of Plymouth Plantation.

Samoset saw the fearful looks on the faces of the colonists. The men hurried to grab their muskets. The women shooed their children into the few houses.

Quickly Samoset threw up his hand in greeting. He called out in English, "Welcome, English!"

The settlers looked surprised to hear the Indian speak English. But they also looked relieved. At last they put down their muskets and welcomed him.

The Pilgrims had many questions for Samoset. Sometimes he had trouble understanding their rush of English words. Sometimes he could not find the words to say what he meant. But somehow they managed to communicate.

Samoset explained to the Pilgrims that the place where they had settled was once called Patuxet. He told them the sad story of how the Patuxet people had died in a plague two years earlier. Now the colonists understood why the land was already cleared and ready for planting when they arrived.

Samoset had such a good time that he refused to leave. The Pilgrims tried to lodge him on the *Mayflower*, but the wind was bad. So he slept in Stephen Hopkins's house. But they watched him, for still they did not trust him. The next day Samoset said good-bye to the Pilgrims and returned to Pokanoket.

Proudly he showed the others the presents the English had given him: a fine knife, a bracelet, a ring, an English hat, a pair of stockings, shoes, and a shirt. Then he told Chief Massasoit all that he had seen and all that the English people had said.

Massasoit was pleased. Now he felt ready to visit the English himself. He would take many of his people with him. Everyone would dress in their finest skins and paint their faces in red or yellow or white. Massasoit would wear a beaded necklace of bone around his neck.

Massasoit again sent Samoset to announce his arrival. But this time he sent Tisquantum, too.

Peacemaker

Tisquantum stood on a hill covered with wild grasses and looked down at what used to be his home.

There was a brook below, and across from it was the English village. The people moving about the settlement were dressed much the same as Tisquantum had seen in England. But of course their village was much smaller and simpler than the grand city of London. Near the beach stood one large long building. A few smaller houses were grouped close together, and a dirt street had been formed in front of them. These were plain wooden buildings with sloped roofs of reeds. Smoke curled from a small chimney at one end of each house.

How different these homes were from the round wetus that had stood here when Tisquantum was a boy. The English built fireplaces against the walls of their houses. That way, most of the heat flew up the chimney and through the wall, while the white people shivered in the cold rooms. The Indians, on the other hand, had built fires in the center of their round wetus. That way, most of the heat stayed inside and kept the whole house warm.

But now the wetus were gone. The English lived here. And it was time for Tisquantum to take them Massasoit's greeting.

He and Samoset and three other men carried animal skins to trade. Going down the hill, they crossed the brook and walked into the village.

The English smiled at them. When Tisquantum greeted them they seemed pleased to hear him speak in English.

Tisquantum told the settlers that the Pokanoket's big chief, Massasoit, wished to meet with the leader of the English. He turned and pointed away from the village. Massasoit and sixty men stood proudly at the top of the hill for the English to see.

The Pilgrims were careful. To them, the Indians looked very fierce. They told Tisquantum they were not willing to send their leader, Governor

John Carver, up to the band of Indians on the hill.

Tisquantum hurried back to Massasoit with the Englishmen's words. Massasoit gave Tisquantum a new message for the English. He wanted them to send another man to meet with him.

The Pilgrims talked among themselves. At last they agreed. They would send Edward Winslow, a Saint, with a message of peace from Governor Carver.

To show the Pilgrims' good will, Winslow would offer the Indian chief a pair of fine knives and a copper chain with a jewel in it. To the chief's brother, Quadequina, the Pilgrims sent a knife and a jewel to wear in his ear. They also sent some English food.

Tisquantum led Winslow back across the brook and up the hill. He watched the young white man as he approached the group of Indians with painted faces. Tisquantum knew how it felt to leave the safety of home and go among strangers. He knew Massasoit's men were as foreign to Winslow as the crowds of London had once been to him.

Massasoit stood proudly as Edward Winslow came before him. He was delighted by the gifts. He listened with respect as his white visitor spoke. Tisquantum translated Winslow's words into the Wampanoag language.

Winslow told Massasoit that the leader of all the English, King James, sent greetings of love and friendship. The governor of Plymouth Plantation, Governor Carver, wished to meet with Massasoit to make peace.

Massasoit smiled and nodded at the speech. He ate some of the English food, then gave the rest to the other Pokanoket. He admired the visitor's fine sword and shiny armor. Tell him I want to buy the sword, Massasoit told Tisquantum. Nervously, Winslow let it be known that he would not care to part with it.

At last Massasoit agreed to meet with the Governor in the white men's village. He would take twenty of his men, but they would leave their bows and arrows behind. To ensure Massasoit's safety, Winslow must stay behind as a hostage.

Tisquantum then led Massasoit and the Pokanoket men down into the village. Captain Miles Standish and his men held seven Indians as hostages to ensure Winslow's safety. Then the other Indians were led to an unfinished house where a green rug and several pillows had been laid on the floor.

Soon Governor John Carver came inside the house. He bowed and kissed Massasoit's hand. Massasoit did the same. Then they sat down.

The two leaders had different ways of showing their friendship. Massasoit shared a pipe full of tobacco with the Englishmen. Governor Carver gave Massasoit a glass of "strong water." It was liquor like brandy.

Then it was time to talk of peace. Word by word, Tisquantum translated Massasoit's Wampanoag words into English. Carefully he listened to the English words and repeated them in his native tongue to Massasoit.

At last, with Tisquantum's help, the Pilgrims and the Pokanoket made a peace treaty. They agreed that neither people would hurt the other. Anyone who did was to be turned over for punishment. Each side agreed to help the other if some third group made war on them. Each side agreed to leave their weapons behind when they visited the other's village.

The Pilgrims wrote down the treaty in words on paper. Since the Pokanoket people did not have a written language, for them the treaty was sealed with gifts and speeches.

Everyone seemed pleased with the peace treaty. It would last for more than fifty years.

When the meeting was over, Governor Carver walked with Massasoit and his men to the brook. They embraced each other and said good-bye.

The Pilgrims kept their Indian hostages and waited for Winslow's return. Instead they received word that now Massasoit's brother, Quadequina, was coming for a visit. Soon he came with twenty men. He disliked the Pilgrims' guns and asked that they be put aside. The Pilgrims put them away and then entertained Quadequina as they had his brother.

Finally Quadequina went back to the hill. Winslow was returned and the Pilgrims released their Indian hostages.

Massasoit was pleased with Tisquantum's work in helping to make peace with the English. To show his appreciation, he gave Tisquantum his freedom. Now Tisquantum could go wherever he wanted to.

Tisquantum chose to stay at Plymouth.

Home Again

Tisquantum—now called Squanto by the Pilgrims—once again was living in the land of his childhood. But his life had changed so much since the days when he had lived with the Patuxet people.

He had been raised a Wampanoag here. He had learned to hunt in these woods. But he had also lived among the English in their busy, crowded cities. And he had learned their language and customs. He knew both worlds. But they were very different from each other. And so he no longer felt truly at home with either the Indians *or* the English.

Still, Squanto had a special place among the people of Plymouth Plantation. The Pilgrims knew little of how to make a living in a land so different from England. They depended on Squanto to teach them.

The day after the peace treaty Squanto went to work. He took the Pilgrims to the river to fish for eels. First, he stamped in the shallow water until the eels wriggled out. Then he caught them with his hands. Soon he had a handful of eels. They were fat and sweet, and the hungry English were glad to have them.

With the coming of milder weather, the master of the *Mayflower* took the ship back to England. Now the Pilgrims were truly on their own. Hard work and a good harvest were important if they were to live through another winter.

Squanto taught the Pilgrims how to catch the herring that now filled the streams. He told them to gather as many fish as they could. The herring were good for more than just eating. They were also good for farming.

How could fish be good for farming? the Pilgrims wondered.

When it was time to plant the corn seed, Squanto showed them. He told them to plant when the oak leaf was the size of a mouse's ear. He told them the corn would not grow well in the old fields unless fertilized with fish. First he dug a hole and put in two or three herring. Then he covered the fish with soil. For two weeks they must wait for the fish to decay. Then it was time to plant. Counting out four kernels of corn, he put them over the spot where the fish were and covered them with a little mound of dirt. The fish would make good earth, Squanto explained. That would help the corn grow tall. Twenty acres of corn were planted this way.

As Squanto worked, the lessons of his childhood came back to him. He taught them the ways of the animals of the forest so they could catch them more easily. He showed them where to look for wild berries and fruit.

Many of the plants that grew near Plymouth Plantation did not grow in England. Squanto told the Pilgrims which plants were good to eat and which plants were poisonous.

There was still some sickness at Plymouth after Squanto came to live there. In April everyone had been saddened when Governor Carver died. The Pilgrims chose a Saint named William Bradford to be their new governor.

In early July, after the spring planting, Governor Bradford decided it was time to repay Massasoit's

visit. They would thank the sachem for his friendship, renew the peace with gifts—and perhaps find out firsthand how strong in numbers the tribe was. Bradford sent Winslow to act as his ambassador, along with Stephen Hopkins. Squanto was to guide them to the village of Pokanoket and act as translator.

For an entire day they marched westward, single file, through the thick woods. Often Indians ran out for their first glimpse of an Englishman or to trade for trinkets. That night the travelers came to a riverbank where several Indians were fishing. The Indians shared their dinner of fresh fish with the newcomers. Then Squanto, Winslow, and Hopkins slept among them on the riverbank.

When they left the next morning, six Indians went along and helped to carry their things. Throughout the day, as they hiked in the hot sun, they again met many curious Indians. At last, as they shielded their eyes from the setting sun, Squanto pointed in the distance to a village of we-tus. This was Pokanoket, home of Massasoit.

As they walked into the clearing, the excited villagers gathered round their visitors. Massasoit was not there, they said, so a messenger was sent to fetch him.

When he comes, Squanto told Winslow and Hopkins, they should fire their guns as a salute. But when the Pilgrims drew out their guns to load them, the Indian women and children fled in fear. Squanto had to call them back and assure them that the white men meant no harm.

At last Massasoit returned and Winslow and Hopkins fired their guns in an honored salute. Then the great sachem welcomed them into his wetu.

Once seated, Winslow presented Massasoit with gifts from Governor Bradford: a scarlet horseman's coat trimmed in lace, and a copper chain to wear about his neck. Massasoit was delighted and put them on at once.

Then Winslow delivered Governor Bradford's message. He thanked Massasoit for the friendship of his people. The Pilgrims looked forward to continued peace. But there was one other message, a small request. Winslow hesitated. Could Squanto translate it without offending Massasoit?

The Pilgrims had become very busy. To survive the coming winter, they must work hard now to ensure a good harvest. But they were constantly being visited by curious Indians—whole families!—who must be fed and entertained. There was just not enough time for so many visitors. . . . Of course, Massasoit and his messengers were always welcome . . .

Squanto carefully translated Winslow's words. Massasoit nodded with understanding. He would personally see to it that the Pilgrims were no longer bothered by sightseers. Winslow and Hopkins sighed in relief.

Then Massasoit strutted around, showing off his fine gifts. He made a speech, saying that the Indians, too, wished to continue in peace and friendship and would trade their furs to the English.

The Pilgrims waited politely for some dinner. Since Massasoit had arrived late, however, there was nothing to share. But when the sachem and his wife went to bed, he invited his guests to share his wetu. Squanto felt right at home. Winslow and Hopkins tried to make themselves comfortable on the low wooden beds covered with mats. But it was not so easy for these foreigners who were used to English beds. Especially when two more tall Indian men crowded in with them. And while the Indians' low singing lulled Squanto to sleep, it kept the Englishmen awake. Winslow wrote later that they were far more weary from this night than from the long journey they'd made to get there.

They spent another day—and another long night—in Pokanoket. Then it was time to go home. The Pilgrims wanted to get back to Plymouth in time for the Sabbath. But no doubt they were also longing for the comforts of their own food and beds.

When at last they reached Plymouth, they found the colony in an uproar. Those good-for-nothing Strangers, the Billingtons, were causing trouble again.

The father, John Billington Senior, had been the first person punished at Plymouth. He had ignored Governor Bradford's orders and had even used foul language. For that he was put on public display with his neck tied to his ankles.

One of his sons, Francis Billington, was the boy who had set the *Mayflower* on fire.

Now his brother, John Junior, had disappeared. His mother feared he had been snatched by Indians. Pity the poor Indians! some of her neighbors must have thought.

Soon, Massassoit sent word that John Junior was at Nauset.

At dawn Squanto and Captain Standish led a party of ten men in search of the boy. For a whole day they traveled south in the shallop till a storm forced them to come ashore and camp for the night. The next morning they met some Indians looking for lobsters. Their sachem, Iyanough (EYE-YAN-oh), spoke and waved his arms. Squanto translated. John was indeed with the Indians at Nauset—and he was safe!

Iyanough joined the search as the group continued south. At last, as darkness cloaked the forest in mystery, they arrived at the village of Nauset.

The shallop put down anchor in the water. Captain Standish sent Squanto and Iyanough ashore with a message for Aspinet (AS-pin-et), the Nausets' sachem: "We have come for the boy."

Soon several Indians came down to the water and waded out to the boat. They tried to get the Pilgrims to come ashore.

Suddenly Captain Standish ordered his men to stand ready with their guns. He had seen these Indians before.

At First Encounter beach.

The Pilgrims had since learned why these Indians attacked them. It was their corn the Pilgrims had stolen. Captain Standish told Squanto to give them a message: only the Indians who had been wronged could come aboard.

Two Indians climbed onto the shallop. With Squanto translating, Captain Standish told them they had only to travel to Plymouth, and they would be paid for their corn. The Indians agreed to come.

Captain Standish was relieved. But there was more negotiating to be done. For now Aspinet and fifty men had surrounded the ship. They carried no weapons, but fifty-nine men waded up on shore with bows and arrows in hand.

Suddenly one of the Pilgrims let out a shout. A tall strong Indian was wading out into the water— and he had young John Billington on his shoulders! The boy was wearing Indian beads around his neck and looked none the worse for wear. He had been treated well. In fact, he seemed to be enjoying himself.

John Junior was handed over to his father. Then Captain Standish gave a gift of a fine knife to this man and to the Indian who had first found the lost boy.

Later Squanto hurried out from the village with frightening news for the Pilgrims. The Narragansett Indians, enemies of the Wampanoag, had attacked and killed some of Massasoit's men. The sachem himself had been captured! The worried Pilgrims pushed off for Plymouth.

Forty-eight hours later they arrived in Plymouth and learned that all was well—at least for the Pilgrims. Soon, however, a Pokanoket Indian named Hobbamock ran into Plymouth with more bad news. Conbitant, a sachem of Maltapuyst, was conspiring with the Narragansett Indians. Conbitant had captured Squanto and Hobbamock, too, at Namasket, but Hobbamock had escaped. The last thing he had seen was Conbitant holding a knife to Squanto's chest. Conbitant had said that if he killed Squanto, the English would lose their "tongue"— their ability to speak with the Indians.

By now, said Hobbamock, Squanto must surely be dead.

The Pilgrims were outraged. The next morning ten men set out on foot with Hobbamock as their guide. They would avenge the death of their friend.

By nightfall they reached the village of Namasket. Quickly the Pilgrims surrounded a house where Conbitant had stayed. Then Captain Standish and several men burst into the house—but the sachem was not there. Standish demanded to know where he was, but the Indians stood speechless in fear. Through Hobbamock, who could speak some English, Standish told the Indians that his quarrel was with Conbitant and that they would not hurt their women and children. But by now the village was in an uproar. A few Indians were injured trying to escape. The women and children threw themselves at Hobbamock for protection, calling him *Towam*, or friend. The Pilgrims fired their muskets into the air. Someone called out that Squanto was still alive. Quickly, Hobbamock climbed on top of a wetu and began to shout Squanto's name above the noise. Finally Squanto appeared in the crowd. He was indeed alive!

The Pilgrims gathered up all the Indians' weapons, but they promised to give them back the next day. Then they waited through the night.

But Conbitant and his followers had fled into the woods. So Captain Standish left him a message with the other villagers. If Conbitant harmed any who were friends to the English, the Pilgrims would take their revenge.

The Pilgrims had risked war for the sake of their friends Squanto and Massasoit. They had indeed become an important part of their lives.

Many times that summer Squanto guided the Pilgrims through the woods, along the winding Indian trails—and along the equally complicated paths to peace in such unsettled times.

The Pilgrims often heard rumors that the Massachusetts Indians to the north had threatened them. In September, Governor Bradford decided to send a party of men to trade with the Massachusetts and try to make peace with them. Squanto went with them to act as interpreter. When they reached Massachusetts Bay, however, they met a group of Indian women who seemed greatly afraid of them. But then they saw that the Pilgrims meant them no harm. They grew friendly and cooked them a feast of fresh seafood.

Squanto, however, told the Pilgrims they should just take the women's valuable furs and other belongings, for they were bad people who had often made threats against the colony. The Pilgrims answered that they would not harm them simply because they had used threatening words. Only if the Massachusetts *acted* against them would they become enemies.

The Indian women were pleased at how well these English treated them. When the Pilgrims turned to leave, the women traded everything they had—including the skins off their backs. They wrapped themselves in tree boughs, as their visitors got into their boat. The Pilgrims promised the Massachusetts women that they would come back and trade again.

Hard work, warm days, and plenty of food soon brought good health to the Pilgrims. It was a good summer for the young colony. The children ran and played in the sunshine. They had no school yet, but there was still a lot to learn. They stayed busy hunting for nuts and wild berries, carrying water for the kettle, and fetching kindling for the fires.

With each new month, Squanto had new lessons to teach the Pilgrims. Samoset had gone home to his own people in Maine. This meant that Squanto was the main link between the Pilgrims and the Indians. It gave him a place of power and safety, too. The Indians and the Pilgrims both needed him to communicate with each other. Neither side would dare to hurt him.

With Squanto's help, the Pilgrims saw a good harvest that fall of 1621. It was so good, in fact, that they decided to have a big feast.

They would have a Harvest Home celebration, just like in England.

A Time for Giving Thanks

Squanto soon found himself in a flurry of joyous preparation.

Governor Bradford sent four men out to hunt for wild turkey, duck, and geese. Other men went fishing.

The women, too, had their hands full. Only four women had lived through the first winter. It was up to them to do *all* the cooking. There were two kinds of bread to be made—fried in a skillet or baked in the clay oven. Vegetables needed to be picked, and chickens to be plucked. Someone would have to fetch buckets of water. And then there were the prune tarts and the sweetened spiced pumpkin to make.

The Pilgrims would need lots of room for all their guests, for Governor Bradford had invited Massasoit and his men to come share in the celebration. The men rolled out huge barrels and lay wooden planks on top. These long tables were covered with fine linen tablecloths that the women had brought with them from England.

On the day of the feast, everyone rose early. Delicious smells filled the air. The children laughed and sneaked bites of food as they helped the busy grown-ups. There was such happiness and excitement.

The women kept an eye out for their guests as they cooked and stirred and filled the bowls and platters. Had they cooked enough for everybody? they wondered. Suddenly one of the women gasped, and her hands flew to her face in surprise. Everyone turned to look.

Massasoit and the Pokanoket had finally arrived—all ninety of them!

How on earth could the Pilgrims feed so many people?

Fortunately, the Pokanoket were very good guests. They killed five deer to add to the feast. The tables groaned under the weight of all the food. Some one hundred and forty people gathered around on wooden benches. Governor Bradford led the blessing. And then the eating began.

Squanto and the rest of the people at the feast ate from round wooden plates called trenchers. Sometimes two people shared a trencher. The Pilgrims and Indians did not pass food around the table and wait politely for everyone to be served. The meal was more like a picnic, and they all dived right in. Often they ate straight from a platter or bowl. Forks were not yet in common use, so the merrymakers ate with their knives or spoons—or even with just their hands. Everyone laughed and talked as they reached for a taste of this or grabbed for a bite of that.

All the people at the feast had known true hunger. For Indians and English alike, a good harvest could mean the difference between living and dying. To have plenty of food was a blessing. Everyone ate with joy and a hearty appetite.

The Pokanoket had never tasted many of these English dishes before. But Squanto was familiar with just about everything. Every time he went to take a bite of food, someone grabbed his wrist and asked him to explain something.

What is this? an Indian would ask, biting into something delicious.

What word do the English use for this sweet yellow food they spread on bread? someone else would ask, pointing to the butter.

The questions went on and on. Today this feast among the Pilgrims and the Indians is often called the First Thanksgiving. But the people who attended it did not think of it quite that way.

To the Pilgrims a day of Thanksgiving was a quiet, serious day of prayers and long sermons. It was a holy day for giving praise to God for His goodness.

This holiday was not serious. Instead it was three days of food and games and fun—like the annual harvest feasts that had long been celebrated in England. The only time anyone stopped eating was to play games or dance or sleep.

It was a special time. The English and the Wampanoag came from very different cultures. Squanto had helped bring the two groups of people together. Their clothes and words were very different. But their smiles and laughter were the same.

In the future there would not always be such good harvests. Eventually, there would be times when trouble would threaten the peace between the Pilgrims and the Wampanoag.

But for now there was joy and friendship and plenty to eat.

Rivals

The Pilgrims were not as friendly with all the Indians as they were with the Pokanoket. In January of 1622, the Pilgrims received a strange message from the Narragansett Indians. The Narragansett were a large tribe of Indians who lived to the west of Plymouth. They were enemies of the Wampanoag people, and they had grown powerful when the Wampanoag suffered from the plague. The Narragansett chief, Canonicus (kuh-NON-i-kus), was not happy that the Pilgrims were making friends with other Indians in the area. Ties with the white men made other tribes strong, and this he saw as a threat to the Narragansett.

Canonicus sent a messenger to Plymouth Plantation with a bundle of arrows wrapped up in a snake-skin. The Pilgrims had no idea what this meant, but Squanto knew. He explained that it was an act of war—a challenge to the Pilgrims' power.

What should they do? The Pilgrims were not sure.

Squanto's advice was to stand up to the challenge. He thought the Pilgrims should return the snake-skin filled with bullets and gunpowder. This would tell the Narragansett that the Pilgrims did not fear them.

Governor Bradford followed Squanto's advice. But Canonicus would not even allow the snakeskin with bullets into his village. When the Pilgrims heard this they worried that the Narragansett would attack. To protect themselves they decided to build a palisade—a tall, strong fence—around Plymouth. Every night the gates were locked and a guard kept watch.

At about this time, Squanto's friendship with both the Pilgrims and the Indians began to turn sour.

Squanto was unhappy because Massasoit had sent another Indian advisor and his family to live at Plymouth Plantation. This new Indian advisor was Hobbamock—the Indian who had guided the Pilgrims on their trip to Namasket when they thought Squanto had been killed. Like Squanto, Hobbamock could speak English.

All at once Squanto's special place at Plymouth was at risk. Now someone else could guide the Pilgrims through the wilderness and carry important messages between Massasoit and Governor Bradford.

Even worse, Hobbamock came from Pokanoket, Massasoit's own village. He thus had the power of his own sachem—the chief of the Pokanoket people—and of his village behind him. Squanto had neither. He was an outsider—of the lost village of Patuxet. He had only himself to depend on.

Squanto became jealous of Hobbamock. He feared that the other Indian would become more important to the Pilgrims than he was. He grew watchful and secretive. Squanto believed that he would have to be clever if he was to remain the favorite of the Pilgrims.

Once Squanto had worked to build trust between the Indians and the Pilgrims. Now he began to play on their mistrust.

Unknown to the Pilgrims, Squanto began to spread rumors among the Wampanoag Indians. He told the Indians that the Pilgrims kept the plague buried beneath their Common House at Plymouth Plantation. He said they had the power to send it among their enemies.

This wasn't true, of course. What the Pilgrims really kept buried beneath the Common House was not the plague. It was their barrels of gunpowder—which they had no intention of using against the Wampanoag as long as the Indians remained friendly.

But the Wampanoag believed Squanto's lie, and they were terrified. So many of their own people had already died from the plague. They did not want more to be killed. Squanto used their fear to gain the Wampanoag's loyalty. If they gave him presents, Squanto told them, he would see that the English did not harm them.

The competition between Hobbamock and Squanto grew fierce. Sometimes the Pilgrims were not sure if either Indian was being truthful with them.

In the early spring of 1622, the Pilgrims sought to trade with the Massachusetts Indians, who lived to the north. Hobbamock warned the Pilgrims not to go. He feared that the Massachusetts had joined the Narragansetts and were planning to harm the colony. He told the Pilgrims that Squanto had something to do with it, too. Hobbamock swore that he had seen Squanto meeting secretly with other Indians in the forest.

The Pilgrims did not know if what Hobbamock said was true. But they decided to make the trip anyway. If they did not go, the Indians might see it as a sign of fear. The Pilgrims wanted to show that they were strong, not weak. So, at the beginning of April, Captain Miles Standish and ten other men would head north to meet the Massachusetts Indians.

They decided to take both Squanto and Hobbamock as their guides. That way each Indian would keep a watchful eye on the other. And both would work hard to please the Pilgrims. Besides, Squanto would not be likely to help an Indian attack if he risked being killed, too.

On the very day the trading party left Plymouth in their small boat or shallop, the Pilgrims heard yet another frightening rumor. A frightened native ran into a Pilgrim cornfield and shouted out that many Narragansett were on the way to attack—and that Massasoit was with them.

Governor Bradford leaped into action. He fired the cannon three times to call back the shallop. The

Pilgrims had to move quickly. There wasn't a moment to lose!

Luckily, the men on the shallop heard the warning and hurried back to Plymouth. Quickly the Pilgrims got ready for the attack. They waited all through the night with their muskets and cannon. But nothing happened.

Hobbamock did not believe a word of this story. He kept telling the Pilgrims that Massasoit would not break the treaty. Hobbamock would have been told if something were being planned because he was a pniese, one who advised on war matters.

Once again, the Pilgrims were not sure what to believe. Governor Bradford decided to send Hobbamock's wife to Pokanoket to see what was going on. When she got there, the villagers were going about their normal day. No attack was planned.

Hobbamock's wife went to Massasoit and told him the stories of war the Pilgrims had heard. Massasoit was furious. Of course he had not broken the peace. Squanto, he said, must have made the whole thing up to make the Pilgrims mistrust Massasoit. Squanto was jealous of the chief's power over the Wampanoags.

Massasoit sent messengers to Plymouth. He swore his loyalty to the English and to their treaty.

Later he went personally to Plymouth and demanded that they give him Squanto. The troublemaker must be put to death for his evil doings.

Governor Bradford did not know what to do. He didn't want to anger Massasoit. The chief's friendship was necessary to the Pilgrims' safety in their new home. The Pilgrims were angry with Squanto, too. But Squanto had been a good friend to them in the past. He had been their guide in an unknown world.

Governor Bradford told Massasoit that he understood the chief's anger. Squanto did deserve to die. But the Pilgrims needed his services to survive. For their own safety, they wished to spare him.

This made Massasoit very angry. The Pilgrims were breaking the treaty by keeping Squanto from him.

Once again, the chief sent his messengers to Plymouth—this time dressed in war paint. They carried with them Massasoit's own knife. The chief had ordered them to use the knife to cut off Squanto's head and hands and bring them back to Pokanoket as proof of his death. Massasoit sent many valuable beaver skins to Governor Bradford in payment for Squanto's life.

Governor Bradford would not accept the skins. He told Massasoit's braves that he could not take payment for sending someone to die. But he added that the Pilgrims, too, believed in punishing those who had committed a crime. They would turn Squanto over to the Pokanoket.

Governor Bradford called Squanto to him.

Squanto knew why the governor wanted to see him. He could have run away. Instead, he came and stood tall before the English leader. He blamed Hobbamock for his trouble and accused his rival of spreading untrue rumors about him. But Squanto would agree to whatever Governor Bradford decided to do.

The governor was just about to give Squanto to Massasoit's men, who stood ready to kill him.

Just then, a boat was spotted at sea. Governor Bradford thought it might be Frenchmen. He had heard rumors that they might be in league with Massasoit.

Bradford told Massasoit's men that he would not turn Squanto over to them until he knew who was on the ship. The delay angered the messengers. They returned to Pokanoket without Squanto.

The ship turned out to be an English boat which

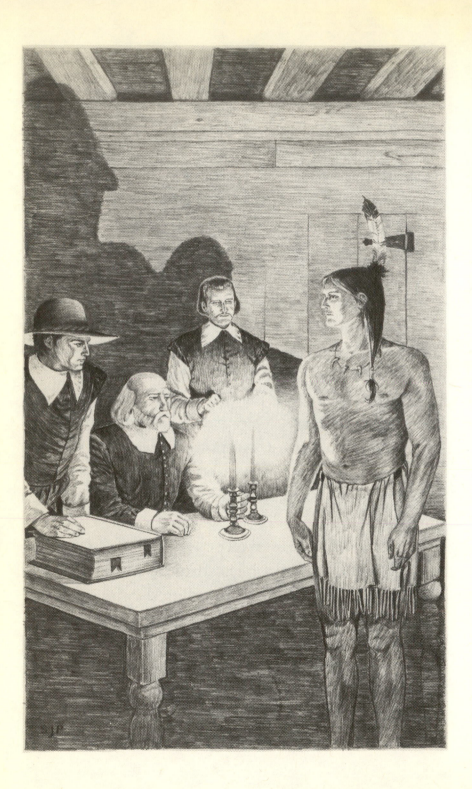

brought new settlers. It was no threat to the Pilgrims. Even so, William Bradford never did give Squanto up.

Governor Bradford had saved Squanto. But after that day, the Pilgrims began to see that Squanto was not being honest. They learned that he sometimes warned the Indians that the Pilgrims were planning to attack. Squanto had told this lie so that the Pokanoket would think they needed him to keep peace with the Pilgrims.

Squanto had been such good friends with the English settlers. Why did he now have a change of heart? Maybe he had begun to doubt the friendship of the English. Maybe he was trying to warn other Indians that the English might one day be a threat to their way of life. Maybe he was jealous of Massasoit's power or angry with the chief for holding him prisoner. It's also possible that Squanto hoped to frighten the Indians who were loyal to Massasoit into coming to him for protection. Then he would be the chief of his own tribe.

Instead, he had cut himself off completely from the Pokanoket. Neither the Indians nor the English would ever fully trust Squanto again. He had hoped to become an important leader. Instead, he had lost almost all of his power, and he had almost lost his life. If the Pokanoket ever caught Squanto, they would kill him. For the rest of his life, he would have to stick close to Englishmen.

So Squanto continued to act as the Pilgrims' guide. In November of 1622, he led Governor Bradford on a trading expedition to Monomoy, also on Cape Cod.

As the Pilgrims got ready to leave, however, Squanto became sick with an "Indian fever." His nose bled. The Indians believed that this was a sign of death. Sure enough, within a few days, Squanto died. He was buried on Cape Cod, near what is now the town of Chatham, only a year after the first Thanksgiving.

Governor Bradford stayed with Squanto to the end. Squanto asked the governor to pray for him so that he could go to the Englishman's God in heaven. The Pilgrims had remained faithful to him. They had protected him. To show his appreciation and love for his English friends, Squanto left all his belongings to the Pilgrims.

Afterword

Tisquantum—called Squanto by the English—lived during a time of great change.

European explorers had come to his homeland, seeking its riches. Whole families came to make new lives there. They forever changed the way of life that the Indians had known for generations.

During the early 1600s, when Squanto was alive, even the richest and most educated people in Europe did not travel far from the towns where they were born. Yet Squanto traveled all the way across the Atlantic Ocean to a land that was completely different from his own.

It was not easy for him. Many of the English looked down on him. They thought he was a "savage." But Squanto learned their language and customs. And he became helpful to the English people in the New World in many valuable ways.

He helped make a peace treaty between the Pilgrims and the Wampanoag Indians that lasted for more than fifty years. He taught the Pilgrims how to survive in their new home—how to fish the sparkling bays and streams and how to grow the precious crop of Indian corn.

Squanto's friendship helped assure that the Pilgrims survived a very challenging time in the founding of Plymouth Plantation. He worked with them to bring in that first good harvest. And they shared their bounty with Massasoit's people in a celebration that has become a symbol of thanksgiving.

At times Squanto worked as a peacemaker and a friend. Other times he acted for his own good.

Squanto was not a perfect, shining hero. He was a real man who did some good things and some bad things. If *he* had not been there for the Pilgrims, some other English-speaking Indian might have played a similar role in helping the Pilgrims to survive. But he *was* there.

He helped bring the Native Americans and the English together in peace. With Squanto's help the

Pilgrims established one of the first permanent English colonies in the New World. Ironically, these were events that would signal the beginning of the end of the Native Americans' way of life.

But all the events of Squanto's life brought him to that very special time and place in American history. They placed him at the center of events that would change the world.

For these reasons, Squanto's story will always be told.

Highlights in the Life of
SQUANTO

late 1500s The American Indian now known as *Squanto* is born in southern New England. He is given the Wampanoag Indian name of *Tisquantum.* The exact date of Tisquantum's birth is unknown.

early 1600s As a young boy, Tisquantum learns how to hunt, fish, and make tools. He spends his childhood in the coastal village of Patuxet, near Cape Cod Bay. By listening to the elders of the village, he also learns the legends and traditions of the Wampanoag people.

During this time, Europeans like Frenchman Samuel de Champlain explore and map Cape Cod Bay. Years after de Champlain's expedition, Englishman John Smith visits the Cape Cod Bay area where he trades with the Wampanoag.

1614 Tisquantum is kidnapped by Captain Thomas Hunt, an English trader and explorer. He is locked in the hold of a ship with nineteen other Indians from his village.

After crossing the Atlantic Ocean, the ship carrying Tisquantum arrives in Malaga, Spain. Captain Hunt puts Tisquantum and the other captives up for sale as slaves. Tisquantum is led away from the slave sale by Catholic monks. It is not known whether these religious leaders rescued Tisquantum or purchased him as a slave. Tisquantum travels by ship to England. He stays in London with John Slany, a wealthy trader. While living with Slany, Tisquantum learns the English language.

1618 John Slany sends Tisquantum to Newfoundland, a large island off the Atlantic coast of Canada. While working for Slany as a translator, Tisquantum meets Captain Thomas Dermer, who takes him back to England. Dermer later introduces Tisquantum to Sir Ferdinando Gorges, an English explorer, who wishes to colonize New England.

1619 In March, Tisquantum sets sail with Captain Dermer and his exploring party for New England. Upon reaching Cape Cod Bay and Patuxet, his former home, Tisquantum is stunned to find his village deserted. He continues north with Dermer's party, then stays behind on the coast of what is now Maine. Tisquantum tries to find survivors of the plague that killed many of his fellow Patuxet.

1620 During the summer, Tisquantum rejoins Captain Dermer as a guide. He is later taken prisoner on the island of Martha's Vineyard by Epenow, who turns him and his fellow translator Samoset over to the Pokanoket chief, Massasoit.

1620 A large ship called the *Mayflower* lands at Cape Cod in November, carrying fifty men, twenty women, and thirty-two children. The ship had left Plymouth, England, two months earlier. On December 26, after weeks of exploration, the Pilgrims land at Plymouth, where they decide to settle.

1621 In an attempt to befriend the English and win them as allies, Chief Massasoit sends Samoset to Plymouth Plantation. He does not want to risk Tisquantum's life on this dangerous mission because he values him too greatly as a translator. Samoset arrives at the Plantation on March 16. After staying a brief time, Samoset returns to the Pokanoket. Tisquantum joins Samoset on a return visit to the Plantation a short time later.

With Tisquantum's help, the Pokanoket make a peace treaty with the English settlers. Tisquantum leads Englishman Edward Winslow to Chief Massasoit. Winslow delivers Governor Carver's wishes for peace. To show his appreciation for this success, Chief Massasoit gives Tisquantum his freedom. Although he can now go anywhere he wishes, Tisquantum chooses to stay in Plymouth.

Tisquantum, now known as Squanto by the English settlers, helps the Pilgrims prepare a feast to celebrate their bountiful harvest. Governor Bradford invites Chief Massasoit and about ninety Pokanoket to be their guests.

1622 Tisquantum leads Governor Bradford on a trading expedition to Monomoy, another site on Cape Cod. While there, Tisquantum becomes very sick. He dies several days later. He is buried on Cape Cod near what is now the town of Chatham.

For Further Study

More Books to Read

Clambake - A Wampanoag Tradition. Russell M. Peters (Lerner Publications)

Dark Pilgrim: The Story of Squanto. Feenie Ziner (Chilton Books)

The First Thanksgiving. Linda Hayward (Random House)

People of the Breaking Day. Marcia Sewell (Atheneum)

Squanto: A Warrior's Tale. Ron Fontes and Justine Korman (Troll Associates)

The Story of the First Thanksgiving. Elaine Raphael (Scholastic)

Stranded at Plimouth Plantation. Gary Bowen (HarperCollins)

Tampaneum's Day: A Wampanoag Indian Boy in Pilgrim Times. Kate Waters (Scholastic)

The Wampanoag. Laurie Weinstein-Farson (Chelsea House)

Videos

The Pilgrims. (Encyclopædia Britannica Educational Corporation)

Plymouth Plantation. (Select Video Publishing)

Thanksgiving Tales. (Society for Visual Education)

Index

104